angel

bella

Love and pink pom-pom cheers to
all the Diva-girls who make my life so fabulous-o...

The sparkly-gorgeous Pink Ladies who visit the website,
read the books and write fabulous-o emails and letters to Lola and I – you rock n' rule!

Mr Fabulousness, Anthony – honouree Pink Lady AND Diva – I heart you!

Team Lola – you turn my words into pretty, pretty pages in pretty, pretty books – LOVE YOU!

Family Divas – Mum, Sheila, Val, Beryl, Vix, Nicky, Anna, Amelia
- I'm lucky to have such amazing women in my world!

The totes inspiring Kandy and Seelena – j'adore!

Team Mizz – you're awesome. Fact.

First published in the UK by HarperCollins Children's Books in 2008
1 3 5 7 9 10 8 6 4 2
ISBN-10: 0-00-726491-7
ISBN-13: 978-0-00-726491-9
A CIP catalogue record for this title is available from the British Library.
Text © 2008 Lisa Clark
Art © HarperCollins Children's Books
Art by Holly Lloyd
Printed and bound in China

Lola Love
Viva la Diva

By
Lisa Clark

HarperCollins *Children's Books*

Introduction

So they haven't made a movie based on your life yet?

That's no reason not to be a starlet in your very own feature film every single day. In fact, I'd highly recommend it because, chica, it's your time to shine!

Yep, you can become a star-shaped diva in your own sparkle-filled world by thinkin' pink, unlocking your superstar potential and A-listing your life!

Viva la Diva has everything you'll ever need to live your life like a true star – you'll uncover your YOU-nique star qualities, create your own glitter-sprinkled luck and live life by your very own set of feisty, fun, fearless and fabulous Viva la Diva rules.

So, what are you waiting for? Roll out the pink carpet, step into the spotlight and demand the star attention you deserve. Because you don't have to be in the movies to become a superstar pink thinkin' diva!

Love and pink glitter sparkles,

Lola xx

Contents

Diva-in-training

Chica, you've just scored yourself a VIP, access-all-areas pass to divadom – a place where you'll always look totally ah-mazing, even when you're just chillin' in your comfy track suit bottoms and a tee. You'll be uber popular too, with lots of gal pals and the ability to talk to anyone - including those oh, so complicated boy types - without tripping over your words. And what's more, you'll always, and I mean always, gets what you want without being rude – so, secure your tiara, practice your air kisses and work your pink-tinted shades because you're about to become a glitter-sprinkled, star-shaped, pink thinkin' diva!

A pink thinkin' diva is NOT, and I repeat NOT, the arrogant, foot stomping, ultra-demanding, hissy-fit throwing type – no, to be a real, sparkly-gorgeous, pink thinkin' diva you will need...

Training for Divadom!

★ **To be self-assured** - You will have total confidence in your sweet self and will be willing to do whatever it takes to feel good about YOU! A pink thinkin' diva does not talk trash about herself and she most deffo does not allow others to make her feel bad.

You will feel totally sophist, independent and glam! You'll heart yourself enough to grab for bigger and better things and you'll speak up and speak out!

Repeat after me: **"I'm me, and I rock!"**

★ **To know your own mind** – You are able to recognise your own fabulousness and don't need to get confirmation from others. You know what your YOU-nique talents are and you use them to live your life totally unlimited!

You believe that you should stand out because you're different, and you will never try to blend. Evah.

Repeat after me: **"I know what I like, and I like what I know!"**

★ **To set your standards high** – a pink thinkin' diva knows what she wants and gets it. If there is something that you truly want, you work hard to get it, and don't let others or niggly self-doubt get in your way.

You're true to yourself, take unconventional routes, ask questions and won't be fearful if you don't have the 'right' education, background or connections.

Repeat after me: **"because I'm worth it!"**

⭐ **To put yourself first** - You make sure that you take care of yourself – inside and out. A pink thinkin' diva is truly Beauty*Licious – you take time out to do things that are important to you and treat yourself like the goddess-girl you are!

You'll open your own doors, grab your own opportunities and work as hard as you can to become the feisty, fun, fearless and fabulous star-girl you are.

Repeat after me: **"I love me!"**

Forget flippin' through the pages of a glossy magazine and wishing you looked like the uber glam airbrushed image staring back at you, instead, throw your manicured hand up in the air, shout 'Viva la Diva' and start livin' your life like a starlet on the silver screen!

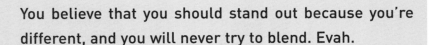

You believe that you should stand out because you're different, and you will never try to blend. Evah.

I
LOVE
ME

Do you go for the best... *or settle for less?*

It's a big, bee-yooo-tiful blast to be all you can be.

Fact.

Do you do what it takes to get what's best for you – or could you be short-changing your sweet self?

Your drama teacher announces she's holding auditions for the school production – are you:
a. So there, sign me up!
b. No thanks, I'm allergic to embarrassment.

A guy you know who isn't your dream dude asks to be your boyfriend – do you:
a. Tell him you're flattered, but you're not into it. You let him know you want to hang with him as your bud though.
b. Say 'yes'. Ok, so he's not perfect – but he's into you.

You and your gal pals want to start an all-girl band. Which instrument are you itchin' to rock out on?
a. Lead guitar. Watch out girl rockers everywhere!
b. Tambourine. It's impossible to mess up in front of an audience.

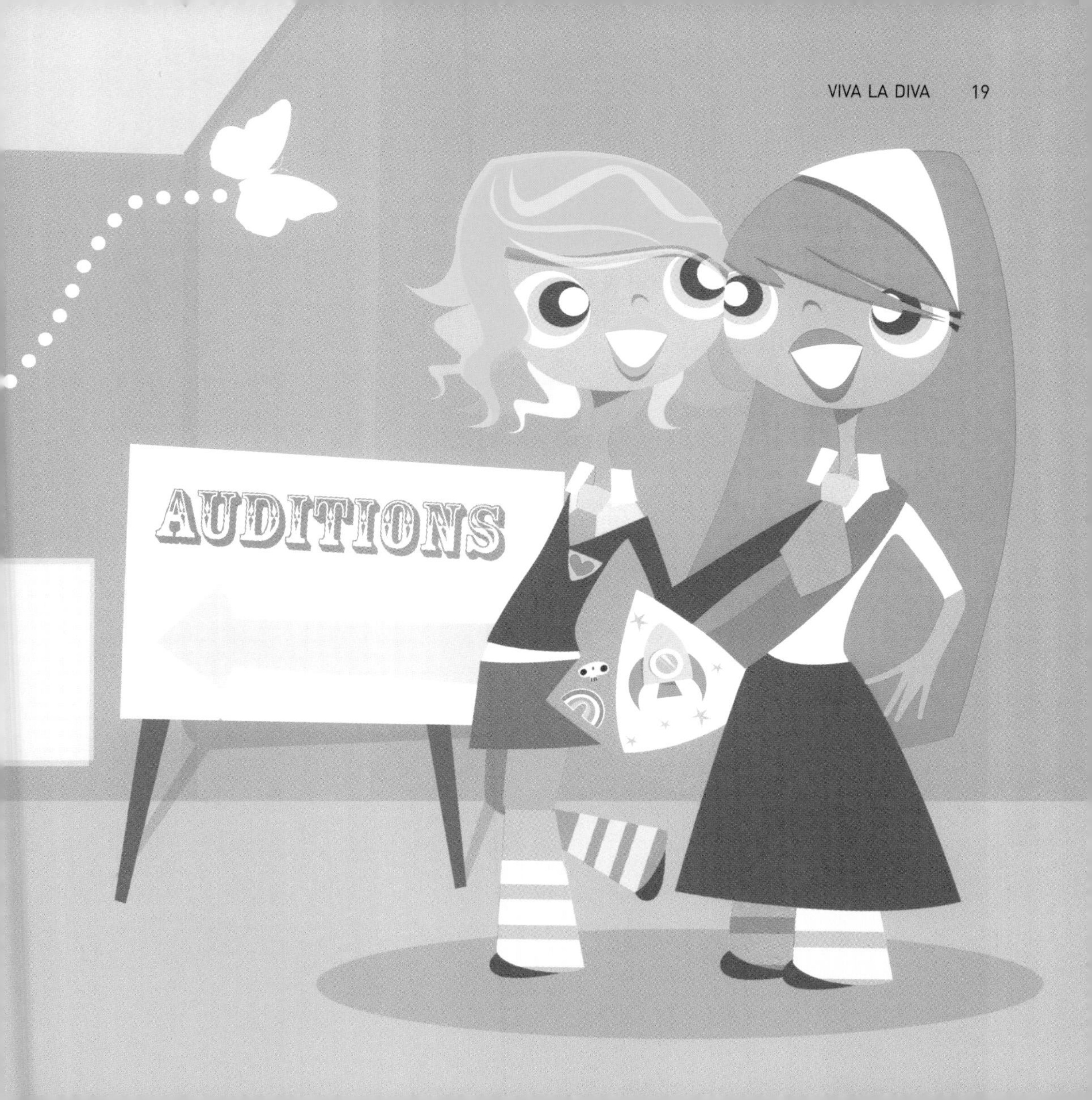
AUDITIONS

Mostly a's

Go Girl – you're most deffo on your way to becoming a pink thinking diva! You go for the awesome stuff life has to offer – because you know you're worth it! When it comes to going for what you want, you never doubt yourself, congrats on the confidence – it'll deffo take you places! Just remember – never get so 'all about me' that you stomp on your buds' feelings, or compete so hard for something that you come off looking super selfish – there's no need to step on anybody's toes on the road to awesomeness.

Mostly b's

You're a really chill chica, and that's admirable. You don't live for the limelight – you're perfectly happy to let others shine. Your plan is to keep expectations low to avoid disappointment if what you hope for doesn't happen. That's a natural instinct – trouble is, it's not much fun, is it? So what if you happen to try something and trip up? You can learn from your mistakes and make it great next time around. You deserve fabulous things chica, so don't settle for life's crumbs. Bite into the whole dee-lish yummy scrummy cookie, sweet thing!

Get into Character

If your life currently feels like a bad movie, it's up to YOU to re-write the script. My life was major-league sucky. In fact, 'til I put on those pink-tinted shades and changed my perspective, I was starring in quite possibly the worst straight-to-DVD movie you have ever seen.

I only had one line and it was 'Poor me.' Pink thinkin' switched my mood from zero to hero, and I realised that it was totally up to me what role I played – this was my movie!

Without a clear sense of your character, who you are and what makes you so unbelievably amazing, your movie makin' is gonna get majorly muddled. So get creative. Imagine that your movie has just been released, you're being interviewed by a super-cute journo boy and he wants to know all about the star of the show... YOU!

Don't hold back, tell him everything!

Cute journo-boy: We haven't seen you on our screens before, could you tell us three things that make you fabulous?

YOU:..

....

....

....

....

....

....

CJB: Who and what do you love with all your heart?

YOU:..

....

....

....

....

....

....

CJB: What makes you laugh?

YOU:..

....

....

....

....

....

CJB: What are you afraid of?
YOU:..

....

....

....

....

....

....

CJB: What are your major accomplishments and achievements so far?
YOU:..

....

....

....

....

....

....

....

CJB: What makes you blush?
YOU:..

....

....

....

....

....

....

Behold the leading ladies!

Girls on film

Calling all leading ladies - a true diva-in-training seeks her character inspiration from the glittering silver screen. Personally, I simply adore the glamorous glamazons: Audrey Hepburn, Marilyn Monroe and Jane Mansfield. They were perma-beauty personified and there really is nothing better than watching ANY of these leading ladies in a back-to-back DVD-a-thon on a rainy day. Sigh.

Inspiro-girls to admire are just a 'play' button away - check out my Viva La Diva playlist...

Viva la Diva DVD playlist

Grease – Better shape up, Pink Ladies style! There's a Pink Lady for everyone to love and adore but personally, I dig on Frenchie. When she has her pink hair phase, natch.
Inspir-o moment: the cropped pants, the flame prints, the bomber jackets – all of which will transform you into a real rockabilly rebel. Are you ready to hand jive, baby?

Xanadu – Ohh-la-la pink leg warmers galore, and a dreamy soundtrack by ELO.
Inspiro-moment: the eternal roller-skating muse that is Olivia Newton John – total fabulousity.

High Society – Like her character, Tracy, Grace Kelly was total high class glamour. Sigh.
Inspiro-moment: Her whole 'look-like-a-good-girl-even-if-you're-not' look. Think neat cardigans and diamante brooches, polka dots, full skirts, lace-trimmed ankle socks and lashings of pink!

Bugsy Malone – There has never ever been a movie like it, and you know how much I heart all things unique!
Inspir-o moment: Make like Tallulah in 20s flapper dresses, Deco jewellery and two-tone shoes. Add flirty frills and feathers and charm the splurge guns off the gangsters!

Pretty in Pink – Words cannot describe how much this film has influenced how much pink there is in my closet! It's the be-all-end-all 80's teen classic. Fact.
Inspiro-moment: Molly Ringworld is the pure essence of pink thinkin' – the official teen queen of pink and pout.

I LOVE Molly!

Your all time favourite flick is

....
....
....
....
....
....
....
....
....
....

What scene in a film deeply inspired you or touched you?

....
....
....
....
....
....
....
....
....
....
....
....
....

Become your own fan club

Chica, it's time to sign up to the most fabulous fan club in the entire world - your own!

You're feisty, fun, fearless and fabulous, that's factuality, so don't spend precious time worrying about who or what you're not, work on who and what you are and be the very best YOU that you can possibly be.

You're a diva-in-training and the good news is that fitting in is not a requirement in divadom.

Why? Because it's hard to stand out while you're fitting in, that's why!

I know that feeling different isn't always comfy, especially when you're a teen girl in the world, but people don't go to the cinema to see 'average', they don't buy concert tix to hear 'typical'. Differences may seem like a disadvantage, but when you're a pink thinkin' diva, you work 'em, sweet thing!

Check out the so-called geek girls who spend whole days in front of their computers. If they're wise, they'll not worry or mope about their lack of invite to a girly get-together. Instead, they'll spend their evenings perfecting their knowledge of new technology in order to eventually create a brand new, female-led, whoop-ass version of Apple or Google.

So, inspired by stand-out girls who embrace their YOU-niqueness, think Cyndi Lauper, Kelly O and DJ girl Lauren Laverne, I purposely made myself stand out from the crowd.

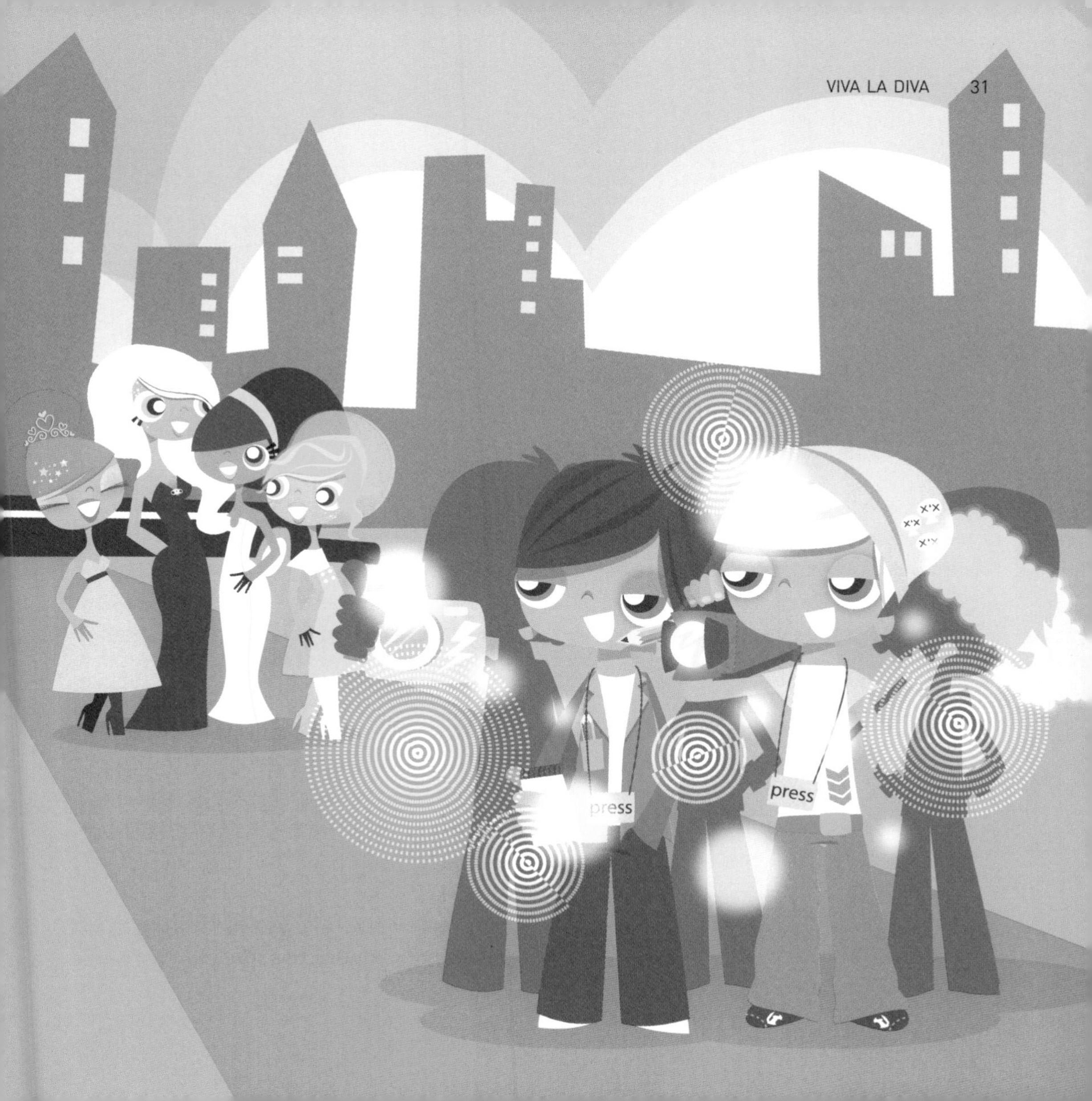
press
press

'Be confident...'

Jeez, before I met Pink Lady, Bella, I was a total blend-in girl. I was practically invisible. But I didn't want to blend in. I really wanted to be more than just the 'weird, writer girl' label that Eva Satine and her clique had given me without my permission. Which is why when Bella suggested transforming my mousey brown locks to true pinkiliciousness, I jumped at the chance!

Finally, my outside reflected my pink thinkin' inside, and I loved what I saw in the mirror – it gave me the complete confidence to be the best version of me ever!

Bella says: 'BE CONFIDENT, BECAUSE WHEN YOU HAVE AN AURA OF CONFIDENCE, YOU ATTRACT ATTENTION AND BEFORE LONG, OTHERS START SEEING YOU THE WAY YOU WANT THEM TO SEE YOU.'

When you're a pink thinkin' diva – you don't have to be perfect-o, you don't have to be cookie-cutter cute either... So if you don't have to be thin, tall or beautiful, what do you have to be? Confident, of course!

Be Brilliant!

If your crush doesn't know you exist or you constantly compare yourself to pouty-faced model types, chances are your self-esteem is taking a serious bashing.

Hello? You rock!

So instead of fretting about the size of your bee-hind, shake it on the dance floor, because it's time to go from invisible to invincible and become a smart, confident, kick-butt queen!

Body talk

Believe it or not, your body can speak as loud as the words you say, so show people you've got it going on without ever saying a word.

How? With body language of course!

What you say with your body is just as important, if not more so, than what comes out of your mouth. So, if you look like a doormat, people will walk all over you and if you try to blend into the woodwork, people will take your cue and ignore you. The good news is you can transform yourself from doormat to diva by following these simple body talk techniques...

Walk tall: pull those shoulders back, tilt your chin ever-so-slightly up and walk like you're proud of who you are – soon enough you actually will be.

Make eye contact: Nothing screams 'low confidence' more than someone who doesn't make eye contact, so drag your gaze off the floor and look people directly in their eyes. It's a great way to show your interest and they'll be sure to send good vibes back your way.

Unfold your arms: Folding your arms in front of you or slouching is a dead giveaway that you're unsure of yourself. Use your arms and hands to make you seem super enthusiastic – wide hand gestures show openness and small hand gestures can emphasise what you're saying.

Take care not to over-use them though, you don't want to scare people away!

Speak up: If someone asks you, "What did you say?" more than once a day, chica, it's time to pump up the volume! Project your voice when you speak or it will seem like you're not even there.

Try this sound check: put cotton wool in your ears and talk out loud. If you can't hear yourself, speak up!

looking into guitar
boys eyes is great!

Deal with it!

If you're not feeling completely confident yet, the Pink Ladies and I have put together these fail-safe techniques to help you tackle your confidence breakers and ooze self-esteem whatever the situation...

Confidence breaker: "I DON'T LIKE THE WAY I LOOK"
What is it you really don't like? Is it your eye colour? A pimple breakout? The way your hair won't ever do what it should?

Well, there's some stuff you can change – for instance, if your hairdo is getting you down, go to a good salon for a consultation. The stylist will be able to advise you on how to keep your hair looking fabulous. If it's something more permanent, like your freckles or your height, then it's all about loving what you've got, sweet thing!

Comparing yourself to others is a fast track to Doomsville. A place that pink thinkin' divas DO NOT want to visit. Accept yourself for who you are, even your worst bits, and learn to love what's great about you!

Confidence Breaker: "I'M NOT CLEVER"
Don't believe you!
Okay, so you might struggle with those pesky fractions or hate spending time in the art room, but you're probably a super star on the hockey pitch or kick-ass at writing essays. The key to surviving school – and having a brilliant career at the end of it all – is finding your top skills and working on them. So if you love writing, get a short story published in the school magazine. Or if French is your thing, find out if there's a foreign exchange you can go on. Building up your self-esteem in the classroom will get you noticed for all the right reasons – go girl!

Confidence Breaker: "I'LL NEVER GET A BOYFRIEND"
Hold it! Are you one of those girls who think their lives would be perfect if only they had a guy on their arm?

Forget it! While boy-types are nice to look at, a sure-fire way to feel super confident is to hang out with your Pink Ladies doing the things you love to do. When you're good to yourself, your confidence will soar and you will turn the heads of cute dudes on a regular basis.

Make yourself feel fab all day long...

Be nice to you: Being mates with yourself is the first step to feeling confident. Run yourself a bubble bath, tell yourself you're fabulous every day, watch your fave DVD on repeat, dance around your room to your favourite tune – anything that makes you feel the star-shaped sparkle girl that you actually are.

Think good thoughts: When you're feeling like a nervy girl, force your mind back to a situation when you felt glitter-girl-great – like the time when you laughed out loud with your Pink Ladies 'til your tummy hurt. Remembering good times will give you an insta-confidence boost.

Control your destiny: You, and only you, Miss Fabulous, can get new things going on in your life, so haul yourself off the sofa, become Action Girl and make it happen. Putting something off, or worse still, doing nothing at all, will only stress you out and slow down your confidence trip. Not good.

The Viva la Diva pink thinkin' challenge!

If you have a negative thought... replace it with an IPR – an Instant Positive Replacement.

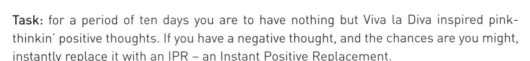

Here's a 10-day pink thinkin' challenge for you, Pink Ladies!

Task: for a period of ten days you are to have nothing but Viva la Diva inspired pink-thinkin' positive thoughts. If you have a negative thought, and the chances are you might, instantly replace it with an IPR – an Instant Positive Replacement.

For example:

Negative thought: 'I'LL NEVER GET ALL THIS HOMEWORK DONE!'
Instant Positive Replacement: 'The sooner I get it done, the sooner I can watch TV!'

Negative thought: 'I'LL NEVER BE ABLE TO DO THIS CHALLENGE'
Instant Positive Replacement: 'Well, I might make half an hour, and that's a lot better than I normally do!'

Ten-day challenge

Keep notes throughout your ten-day Viva la Diva pink thinkin' challenge:

What are some of your negative thoughts? How does being positive make you feel?

....
....
....
....
....
....

What are your IPR's?

....
....
....
....
....
....

How does being positive make you feel?

....
....
....
....
....
....

Bad thoughts

If you have a bad thought, don't worry or beat yourself up about it, just change it.

Now, if you can't think of a positive thought, or you can't be bothered or motivated to, well, no worries, you just go right back to day one and start the sparkly-gorgeous 10-day-challenge all over again!

How great would it be if, for the next ten days, no matter how you feel, no matter what's going on in your life, you had ten whole sunshine-filled days without dwelling on a negative thought? How fabulous would that be? Go on, try it, I dare you!

Not only will this pink thinkin' perma-positivity affect you, but it'll affect the lives of those around you too. Watch how your parentals eyes light up when you smile and give a full-on positive Viva la Diva response. Use when the skies are cloudy or your teach is going mad!

Viva La Diva Tip: If you've been beating yourself up for a long time, it might feel really uncomfy to suddenly flick your mood switch to 'positive' and be a more pink-thinkin' person. Sometimes it might feel like you're even faking it. Well, that's okay, because to begin with we are faking some of our sweet-self-talk, but the more we tell ourselves, the closer we get to actually becoming that fabulous-o person we really are.

Cool, eh?

Bad days

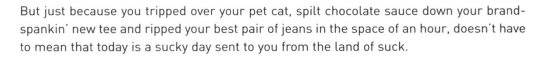

Bad things do happen, even to pink-thinkin' divas.

Rude and wrong, but unfortunately, fact. Grr.

But just because you tripped over your pet cat, spilt chocolate sauce down your brand-spankin' new tee and ripped your best pair of jeans in the space of an hour, doesn't have to mean that today is a sucky day sent to you from the land of suck.

In any situation, however bad you may think it is, a pink-thinkin' diva will always do the following:

> ### 1. Keep cool.

> ### 2. Ask herself some problem-solving questions – instead of asking 'why is life so unfair?' and committing herself to a day without sunshine, she asks questions that could give her useful answers like, 'why is this not working?' or 'what can I do to make this better?'

> ### 3. Realise that it could have been a whole lot worse, laugh about it and move on.

Script Prompter

"...THE BEST FASHION ACCESSORY IS A GOOD BOOK... AND HIGH-HEELED SHOES... I LIKE THEM AS WELL..." **Vivienne Westwood**

Reading is cool.

Fact.

Especially when it involves reading butt-kickin', inspir-o books to help with your very own super-fabulous script for life.

Bella's script prompter - Tall Tales by Jerry Hall
You might know her as Mrs Mick Jagger, but to me, she's as iconic as any silver-screen film star. Not only is she the woman I most like to look at, but she is brilliant as well! Her pals have included Salvador Dali and Andy Warhol – how cool? This book is my inspir-o bible... I carry it around in my bag and read quotes from it when I'm in need of some insta-glam.

Jerry grew up in a trailer park and when she was eighteen, her mum saved up to buy Jerry a one-way ticket to Paris, so she could follow her dream of becoming a star. Armed with only a Fredrick's of Hollywood gown and a string bikini, she made her dreams come true! She gave me hope that a girl like me can be noticed by using her personality and by standing tall on her own two marabou mules. I heart Jerry mostest!

Sadie's script prompter: Any book about Marilyn Monroe
She's history's most vulnerable, inimitable, irreplaceable angel of glamour. In a sea of Oscar winners, nobody shined as brightly as her.

J'adore!

Angel's script prompter: Edith Head's Hollywood
Edith was the most legendary of all movie wardrobe mistresses. She was, at one time, more famous than the actual celeb-types she dressed. In fact, her office became a star attraction on the Universal Studios tour in the '70s. Some of the girls she so breathtakingly dolled up were...Grace Kelly, Liz Taylor, Audrey Hepburn, Sophia Loren, Mae West, Bette Davis and Natalie Wood...to name only a fraction of her sparkly-gorgeous client list – a must for any fashionista!

My script prompter: It's so hard to choose just one, but I'd say any book about Jane Mansfield
Star of The Girl Can't Help It...Jayne was a va-va-voom blonde who lived in a Beverly Hills mansion dubbed the 'Pink Palace', a heart-shaped swimming pool, she would take her pet leopard for daily walks down Hollywood Boulevard, drove the only pink Cadillac in LA, while housing an impressive IQ of 163 in her seemingly bubbly beehive. Now that's what I call fabulous!

Jayne was, to put it in her own words..."SIMPLY DE-VOOM!"

What books are your script prompters?

....

....

....

....

....

....

....

....

....

Sweet talkin' gal

True pink-thinkin' divas whisper sweet nothings to themselves on a daily basis – if I ever catch my reflection, I'll give myself a cheeky wink and say 'why, Lola, you look really rather ravishing today' in a I'm-in-an-old-school-movie kind of way.

Pay yourself a compliment, pronto!

....

....

....

....

They also hand out compliments like they're candy-covered treats – if you see someone with a bag you dig, tell them. Or if your best bud is looking amazingly ah-doreable, let her know!

Prepare a compliment for your best bud, she'll love you for it!

....

....

....

....

But most importantly, a pink thinkin' diva accepts and collects compliments like a celeb-type collects oversized, overpriced handbags. When someone says something nice to you – don't downplay it or brush it off – just smile and say thank you – it's the absolute Viva la Diva thing to do!

What's the best compliment you've ever been given?

....

....

....

....

Tough talkin'

Do you ever feel like everyone wants something from you? And even though you want to say no, you actually say yes?

It's because you're afraid you'll hurt their feelings, right?

Look, it's mucho important to be a nice person, but sometimes people will take advantage of a sweet-girl nature and will walk all over you if you let 'em. Grr.

The trick is not to let 'em.

Bella believes that it is absolutely possible to kick butt when you need to, in the nicest possible way, of course – check out her 'how to talk tough in any sitch' tips of fabulousity!

Borrow-happy friends

They beg to borrow cash, or the cute-as-a-button new leopard-print pumps that you haven't even worn yet, so you let them.

How to deal: If your friend still hasn't paid you back from the last time you lent her cash, and now she's asking again, or if your stuff keeps getting returned with stains – or not at all – and you feel completely taken advantage of, it's time to draw the line. If you don't, you'll end up resenting your friend.

Try saying: "I PROMISED MYSELF I WOULDN'T GIVE ANY MORE LOANS UNTIL PEOPLE PAY ME BACK." or if it's an item of clothing or a dvd, say: "I KNOW YOU'D BE CAREFUL, BUT I'VE DECIDED NOT TO LEND IT TO ANYONE. I HOPE YOU UNDERSTAND."

If she's a real friend, she totally should.

Agony aunt

You're a good listener and love helping your friends out, but lately you feel like their very own personal agony aunt.

How to deal: If your mates' problems are getting you down, it's time to let 'em know. It won't make you a bad person, it will just stop you getting allsorts of crazy-mad with them.

Don't stay on the phone for hours when you don't feel like it, just say: "I'M SORRY BUT I HAVE TO GO – CAN I CALL YOU TOMORROW TO SEE IF YOU'RE OK?" Learn to start saying how you feel. Being honest isn't the same as being nasty. Friendship is about give and take and you shouldn't have to do all the giving. Being strong will earn you mucho respect.

Gossip girls

Get-togethers with your gal pals are starting to resemble the four-way phone conversation between The Plastics in *Mean Girls*.

How to deal: When mates pressure you to be mean about a mutual friend who's not there, it can be hard not to join in – even though you know it's wrong. But remind yourself, if they bitch about her, they'll probably bitch about you too. That should make it easier to make a stand. The simplest way to protest is to say nothing. That way you'll have a clear conscience without losing face. But if you feel brave enough to say something, just say you'd rather not get involved.

Lil' miss let down

Your friend is so much fun to be with but you can't rely on her for anything. She's always late to meet you, forgets your birthday every year, and you're totally inseparable until a guy comes along, and then you don't see her for dust...

How to deal: A friend like this is rarely doing it to be mean. Usually, it's because you're letting her get away with it. So stop making excuses for her and don't accept a half-hearted apology.

Next time she upsets you, don't say: "IT'S OK," say, "ACTUALLY, I FEEL LET DOWN. IT'S NOT GOOD ENOUGH AND I WOULDN'T DO IT TO YOU. PLEASE DON'T DO IT AGAIN."

She won't change overnight and you might need to say it a couple of times before you get results, but if you make it clear your friendship needs to be earned, she should start to make more of an effort.

Friendship is about give and take and you shouldn't have to do all the giving. Being strong will earn you mucho respect.

Talk tough, chica!
Turn people down without letting them down.

Speak up – When you want people to take you seriously, say it like you mean it. This way people will know that no means no and will be less likely to persuade you to say yes.

Be clear – When turning someone down, use 'I' phrases like "I FEEL..." or "I THINK..." so they know it's a choice you're making for yourself and not against them.

Don't apologise – Don't feel like you ever have to apologise for saying no. Never say sorry for staying true to what you want.

Make a note of all the situations you think you could deal with better, and how you normally react. After each one, write a sentence about what you're going to say, or how you're going to deal with it, next time it happens – you'll be totally prepared and not fluff your lines!

....

....

....

....

....

....

....

....

....

....

....

....

....

....

....

....

....

....

....

....

....

....

Stage presence

Do you have stage presence? Do heads turn when you walk into a room?

While you may not want to rock out on a stage like Bella, or strut down a catwalk like Angel – a pink-thinkin' diva should always be able to step into the pink-tinted spotlight and work it. The good news is, you don't have to be big-headed or arrogant to come across as confident and happy – no siree.

Check out the Pink Ladies; we all thrive on attention and, like every good pink thinkin' diva should, we demand attention when we walk into a room, but we're never, ever rude and we most deffo have our glitter-girl egos completely in check.

Follow our Viva la Diva pink-glitter-sparkle steps to get the attention you deserve without screaming 'look at me'...

pink ladies getting some attention!

Attention, please!

Get the attention you deserve by having stage presence.

★ Being a loud mouth isn't a necessity - show people what you're about, rather than shouting it in their faces.

If you rock at designing outfits, don't keep talking about it, make a killer ensemble and work it at the school prom. Don't waste your creative energy talking about what you're going to do. Chica, just do it!

★ It may be tempting to try and bluff your way through a conversation. But if you don't know much about the subject being discussed, you'll get mucho more kudos if you listen up and ask questions.

You can't lose – get your facts right and people will respect your wisdom; ask questions and people will appreciate your interest and honesty.

★ Tone down your gossip factor – this will show that there's more to you than people may think. Your mates will trust you with their secrets and your reputation will sky rocket.

Gossiping gives out icky negative vibes. Girl, don't do it.

★ Choose things that you love doing, and not because everyone else is doing them. If you're passionate about something, and enjoying it, you'll have more energy and people will be so much more attracted to you.

★ Most importantly, be yourself. It's a pink-thinkin' fact, everyone is an individual and that's what makes you who you are, gorgeous girl.

Be proud of why you're different, because if you love yourself up, other people will love and adore you too!

Act up!

Becoming a pink thinkin' diva isn't that hard when you know how.

Take Beyonce for instance – on stage, B becomes an alter ego called Sasha, a girl who is totally confident and self-assured.

I love that idea!

Why don't you do the same?

If you don't feel mucho filled-to-the-brim with star-girl confidence just yet, think about the girl you would be if you did have that confidence – what is she like? How does she act? What would she wear? I'm guessing she's pretty fabulous, right?

So today, imagine that you're her.

Give her a name.

Start being as happy as she is, start walking tall, smile.

What you put out, chica, will bounce right back at'cha. If you walk around with a gloomy face, moaning about how unfair life is – people will feel drained when they're around you and will avoid you at all costs.

Instead, beam out fabulousness, beam out smiles, beam out compliments and pink glitter-filled thoughts – it'll come back to you x 100. Promise!

Beyonce as
Sasha

Channel your inner rock star!

If you were to look up super-cool music girls in the dictionary, you'd find pictures of Debbie Harry, Pink, Chrissie Hynde, Cyndi Lauper and Gwen Stefani – well, you would if you looked in Pink Lady, Bella's book, anyway!

Maybe you might have other pop, rock or superstar types, but whoever you're lovin', they all have one thing in common... the Viva La Diva star-quality 'IT' factor.

Bella knows all about the Viva La Diva 'IT' factor. She's a gee-tar playin', rock chick who has to work her confidence every time she steps on stage. She knows the Viva La Diva 'IT' factor is what makes her hero-girls the superstars that they are.

The good news?

Well, according to Bella, you can work your very own Viva La Diva 'IT' factor by channeling your inner rock star!

Be YOU-nique

There are so many sheep-like people out there who all do, say, dress and eat the same things that being totally original is pretty rare. But, when you dig yourself and, instead of hiding the thing that others might think is odd or different, you emphasise it – that really is a sure sign of superstar behaviour!

Own the stage (or just the classroom!)

You can just tell by the way a person walks up to the microphone if they have star quality. It's the way they look out at the camera or the crowd before they've even played or sung a note – you can do the same in the classroom. Make like a rock girl by walking tall and making eye contact with all your classmates.

Don't be so serious

When you have a sense of humour about yourself and everything around you, you become insta-attractive girl. There's no need to be a full-on comedian to stand out, just be someone who is bubbly in spirit and humour.

Rock out like a rock-girl

If you're done channeling and really, really wanna be a rock girl, you need to get writing the coolest forms of poetry: a song!

Bella's simple song-writing rules

Be ready.
Always have a mini-tape recorder or a pen and notebook with you. When inspiro hits, sing or jot down your idea ASAP.

Be different.
Writers use a lot of the same imagery and words; challenge yourself to explain things in new ways.

Don't throw anything away.
A lyric or tune that doesn't work now could be the perfect fit for a song you write later! So keep it somewhere safe!

Don't force it.
Don't focus on writing a hit song or push yourself to write when you're not feeling it. The best songs come naturally. Honestly!

Learn at least one instrument.
Whether it's the guitar, piano or even your voice, instruments help you to express yourself, which makes writing songs easier. So go on, take some lessons!

Charm School

Have you ever wondered why some girls just seem to totally rock n' rule whatever they do?

Not in an Eva Satine way. I mean, sure, she's popular, she's got canteen groupies and she's stepping out with the totally crushable jock boy Jake, but, she has icky, nasty insides and no matter how cool she thinks she is, that will always make her major league un-pretty.

No, I mean in a super cute Sadie way.

When I first met Sadie, she had customised her school jacket with pin badges that had slogans like: 'I love me' and 'reading is cool', she had a huge killer watt smile and always had a whole bunch of people who wanted to talk to her, even boys.

She's seriously smart and total adoreability on an ice lolly stick, but Sadie says rockin' and rulin' is not about either of those things. In fact, she reckons being the girl that everyone digs is something every girl can become...

"...CHARM IS NOT JUST A CUTE ACCESSORY FOR YOUR SCHOOL BAG, IT'S A GREAT WAY TO CAST A SPELL OF FABULOUSITY OVER EVERYONE YOU MEET!..."

everyone always wants
to talk to Sadie!

> **Look someone in the eyes, then, let a slow smile build up on your whole face...**

Lesson one: Be prepared

Charming people always have something to talk about in every situation, so be prepared. You could carry a conversation piece - an interesting piece of jewellery, a cute bag that you've customised yourself, a pin badge with your favourite slogan or catch phrase – anything that will break the ice or prompt people to ask you about it. When they do, have a little story ready, ("Oh this scarf? Well, funny you should ask actually...") Don't, however, prepare and rehearse actual statements or jokes as you'll sound like an extra from a really, really bad daytime soap opera.

Lesson two: Get Lippy

Your smile is a definite VIP pass to popularity. It makes you appear friendly and enthusiastic and totes approachable. It has to be genuine though – you can't just paint a perma-grin on your face and expect people to fall for it. For pure Viva La Diva magnetism, try the 'spill-over' smile. Look someone in the eyes, then, let a slow smile build up on your whole face as if in response to the genuine affection you're feeling towards them. It'll bag you a sincere smile – not a phoney, instant people-pleasing one.

> **Whether it's a simple brush of your hand or a full-on hug, you'll send love-me waves surging through them**

Lesson three: Touching stuff

Physical contact can work wonders to maximise your bond with someone, whether it's your boy crush or a potential girl bud. Whether it's a simple brush of your hand or a full-on hug, you'll send love-me waves surging through them. Watch their actions too – if they run their hands through their hair, mirror it. It's a sure fire way to build affection. Make it subtle though, you don't want them to think you're mocking them.

Lesson four: Hear-say

The single most important thing you can do to make people dig you is easy – just listen to them! It's a huge compliment to have someone's total attention – gal pals will trust you with their deepest, darkest secrets and parentals and teachers will be blown away with your focus and maturity. Make sure you keep those 'Me's' in check though. It's annoying when people always bring the convo back to themselves. Listening properly involves getting rid of any distractions – so no sneaky texting and no 'uh-huh' uninterested murmurs either, okay?

Your Viva La Diva charm School checklist

Don't risk being a Charm School dropout, here's what you need and how to get it...

Charisma – Love who you are. Stand up straight, move around to appear enthusiastic and lean slightly forward when talking to people and you'll instantly send 'I'm a fab person' waves surging through any room!

Make others feel important – Let people know they matter and you enjoy being around them, develop a genuine smile, nod when they talk, briefly touch them on the upper arm, and maintain eye contact.

Genuine interest in others – Dare to care. Ask after a friend's brother if he's been poorly; ask your teacher how her new puppy is doing. This will show how warm and friendly you are and that you actually remember and care about what's going on in other people's lives.

Generous – You can be generous in lots of ways - if a friend is moving, offer your time to help her pack. If your bestie hasn't a thing to wear on her first date offer her first pick of your wardrobe. Doing good things for others is a win-win sitch, your friends will think you're fab and you'll feel all warm and fuzzy for your good deed.

Most importantly, true charm comes from within, so find ways to be yourself and share your already rather wonderful personality with those around you!

Charisma

Make others feel important

Genuine interest in others

Generous

Be myself

Drama Queen V Pink Thinkin' Diva

Every good movie needs a teensy-bit of drama, but if your life is all about the dramz, chances are you've got a tendency to be a hissy-fit throwin', foot stompin' drama queen. But what happens when it takes over your life?

Ask Angel.

"...BEFORE I WAS A PINK THINKIN' DIVA I WAS TOTALLY GUILTY OF TURNING EVEN THE MOST BORING ASPECT OF MY LIFE INTO A CONFLICT-LADEN MINI-CRISIS. I WAS SCARED THAT MY LIFE WOULD BE POSITIVELY DULLSVILLE WITHOUT IT, SO I'D HAPPILY CREATE MORE THEATRICS THAN A LONDON WEST END SHOW.

IF I GOT A LOW MARK ON AN ESSAY, GRAZED MY KNEE WHILE RUNNING OR WASN'T ABLE TO MAKE A PARTY BECAUSE I'D BEEN GROUNDED, THESE WERE ALL PERFECT-O OPPORTUNITIES FOR THE DRAMA QUEEN IN ME TO THROW A FULL-ON, RED-FACE-INDUCING, HISSYFIT.

ANYTHING THAT SENT SERIOUS SPARKS FLYING WAS JUST WHAT I WANTED.

I THOUGHT THIS CONTINUING QUEST FOR DRAMA KEPT MY LIFE INTERESTING, BECAUSE, WITHOUT THE BLAZING BUST-UPS AND BAD BEHAVIOUR, MY LIFE WOULD BE BORING, RIGHT? WRONG.

LIFE IS ACTUALLY FABULOUS X 100 WITHOUT THE DRAMA, BECAUSE BEING A DRAMA QUEEN IS REALLY, REALLY HARD WORK. FACT. ALL THAT FOOT-STOMPIN' AND SHOUTING CAN SERIOUSLY TIRE A GIRL OUT, Y'KNOW. I ALSO VERY RARELY EVER GOT MY OWN WAY, WHICH KIND OF DEFEATED THE OBJECT. GRR.

NOW, HOWEVER, I'M A PINK-THINKIN' DIVA AND PINK-THINKIN' DIVAS THINK AND ACT A WHOLE LOT SMARTER THAN ANY HISSYFIT-THROWIN' DRAMA QUEEN I KNOW!"

Angel having a hissy fit! Very scary!

Are you a Drama Queen?

If Angel's antics ring alarm bells with you, it's time to reality-check your hysterics.

For sure, a little drama is exciting, but a long-term drama habit can have serious side effects on your life.

To guarantee your movie is a box office hit, check your storyline for its drama content...

☆ **Do you give your parents a hard time? Do you throw your entire house into stressy turmoil, instigating screaming fights and acting ridiculously melodramatic to get your own way?**
Shouting will only ever give you a sore throat and is likely to score you several days grounded in your boudoir. Try not to alienate your parentals.

So they won't let you come in at 9? Instead of foot-stompin', why don't you agree to their suggestion of 8, then after two weeks, ask to renegotiate? This will show how much you respect them and how grown-up you can actually be, and is much more likely to get the result you want.

☆ **Do you create drama out of boredom?**
Are you worried that your performance lacks glitter and sparkle? You don't have to re-write your script by telling over-blown versions of events in order to add fun and excitement to your story line, just do fun and exciting things instead. Join after-school clubs, start a new sport, take up a new activity - soon your life will be so filled-to-the-brim with great stuff, you won't have to go to the trouble of actually making it up!

Angel and her mum get along great now there's no added drama

☆ Your friends are your supporting cast, so treat them well! It's one thing to have the odd melodramatic moment but if you're known for creating conflict just for your own pleasure, it's only a matter of time until people bore of your theatrics. Take time out to listen to them when they're talking and generally be what a good friend should be: supportive, caring and fun to be with!

☆ To make sure your storyline remains drama-free, learn to find a balance between what's really worth fighting over and what's easier to let go. Is it really worth throwing your mp3 player across the room just because you got a bad mark? Do you think screaming at your l'il bro will change the fact that your crush hasn't rung you yet? You might worry that eliminating the drama will make life more boring, but guaranteed it'll make your storyline far more interesting in the long run.

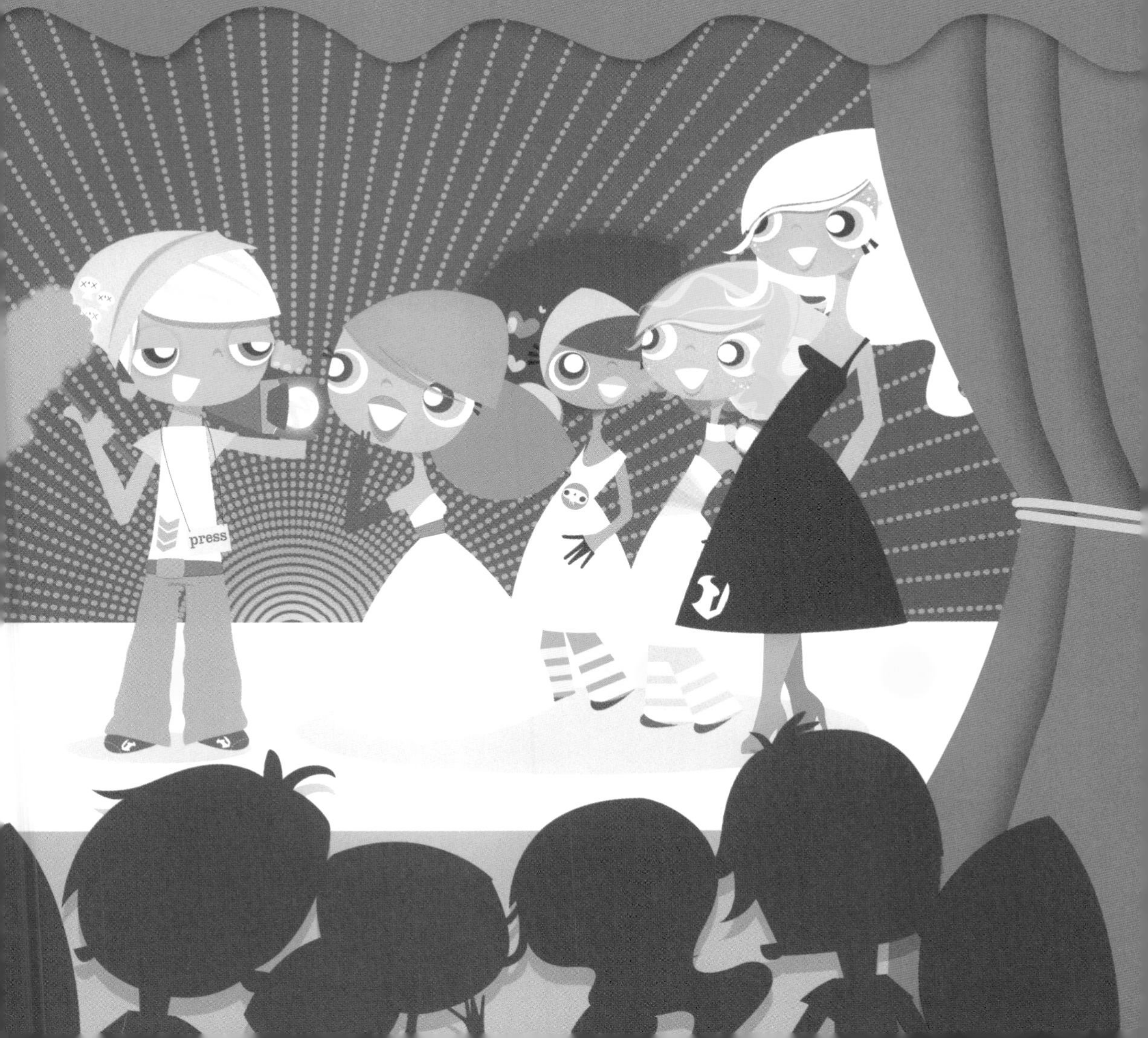
press

Ch-ch-ch-changes

If, like Angel, you wanna change your label, forget new year's resolutions, make new YOU resolutions instead!

If you don't like your hair, change it. If you're in with a bad crowd, make new friends. If you're bored, do something different. If you want to sing, start singing lessons.

You're the writer, director and star of the show and re-invention is a super cool thing to do, check out Madonna, she's the queen of re-invention!

And that whole waiting 'til New Year comes in order to make a change? Well, that's just silly!

Go-for-it! Ever feel like you're just coasting along, doing the same things, going to the same places?

Setting yourself some goals is the pink-thinkin' way to give your life a shake-up.

Start by writing a list of stuff you'd like to achieve – Think big!

So you want to be a netball player? Sign up to be in the school netball team and get practising. You want to go to see your fave band live? Offer to do extra chores to earn money for the ticket.

Your goals can be as hard or as easy as you like – from asking out your crush, learning a new instrument, to making friends. Go it alone, or compare goals with your Pink Ladies. Their support could make all the difference.

Now, work out what baby steps you could take to make them happen.

....
....
....
....
....
....
....
....
....
....
....
....
....
....
....
....
....

Kindness is cool

Pink-thinkin' Divas dare to care.

Fact.

You don't have to do crazy-huge things to make a difference. One little act of kindness can make you feel seriously good about yourself – try it and see. Use your free time to put your good will skills to the test. Why not Sky+ your sis her fave TV programme so she doesn't miss an episode? Or pay your grand-parentals a long-overdue visit?

Being nice has a total snowball effect – take the trouble to be sweet-as-sugar and others will be too because you've given them a positive, pink glitter-filled boost.

making friends with
the new girl at school

Get Crafty

If your school bag is looking major league tattsville, what's a pink thinkin' diva to do? Call on super-cool Laura, the superstar creator of www.heidiseeker.com – home to an infinite amount of sparkly-gorgeous treats – to provide a step-by-step guide to make sure you stand out from the crowd in the playground, that's what!

You will need:
☆ A plain bag
☆ Cheap plastic beads – clash the colours!
☆ Ribbon tied into bows
☆ Needle and thread
☆ Assorted charms, buttons, badges and beads – you can pick up some cute ones from chazza shops to make your bag totes YOU-nique – get thriftin'!

What to do:
1. Using the needle and thread, sew your beads to one corner of your bag.

2. Stitch the ribbon bow over the top and repeat with the other side, leave a loop hanging down for the cute dangly bit.

3. Snip the dangling bit in half, your bag should look something like this...

4. Now for the fun part; using your thread, knot your buttons and charms to your beads, keeping them randomly spaced.

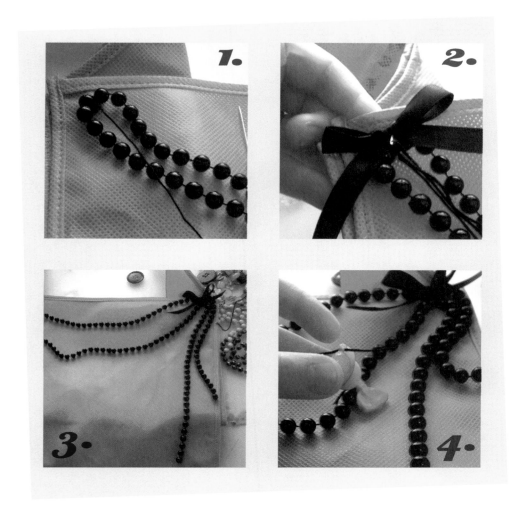

5. Knot them to your beads and secure by doing three double knots.

6. Now pick your fave buttons and stitch in the middle of both your bows.

7. Finally, attach your badges.

HeidiSeeker Tips for Customising

Always place badges in small clusters of odd numbers. They'll look loads better – promise.

Charity shops are often good for picking up unusual bits and bobs to add to your bag – why not try making a cool charm out of old keyrings and odd earrings? Celeb types pay a fortune for customised accessories but, if you unleash your creative talents, your cool 'new' bag will only cost you pennies.

Wohoo – you now have your very own HeidiSeeker-esque bag of wonder!

Choosing your soundtrack

Every movie needs a soundtrack and every leading lady needs a theme tune.

It's Viva la Diva factuality.

Your theme song should be your ultimate inspir-o-girl tune – the song you blast on full volume as you get ready each morning. It should be all about you and who you are right now, at this moment. The lyrics are so about you that you'd swear (except you wouldn't 'coz swearing is so not what pink thinkin' divas do...Our vocab is filled with words of fabulousness, not cuss words) the songwriter used you as their muse-girl. Or maybe the tune just rocks.

Hard.

It should be iconic... like in the opening credits of Pretty in Pink where Molly Ringwald is in her house on the wrong side of town putting together her ah-dorable vintage ensemble and glossing her legendary pout to the Psychedelic Furs tune 'Pretty in Pink.'

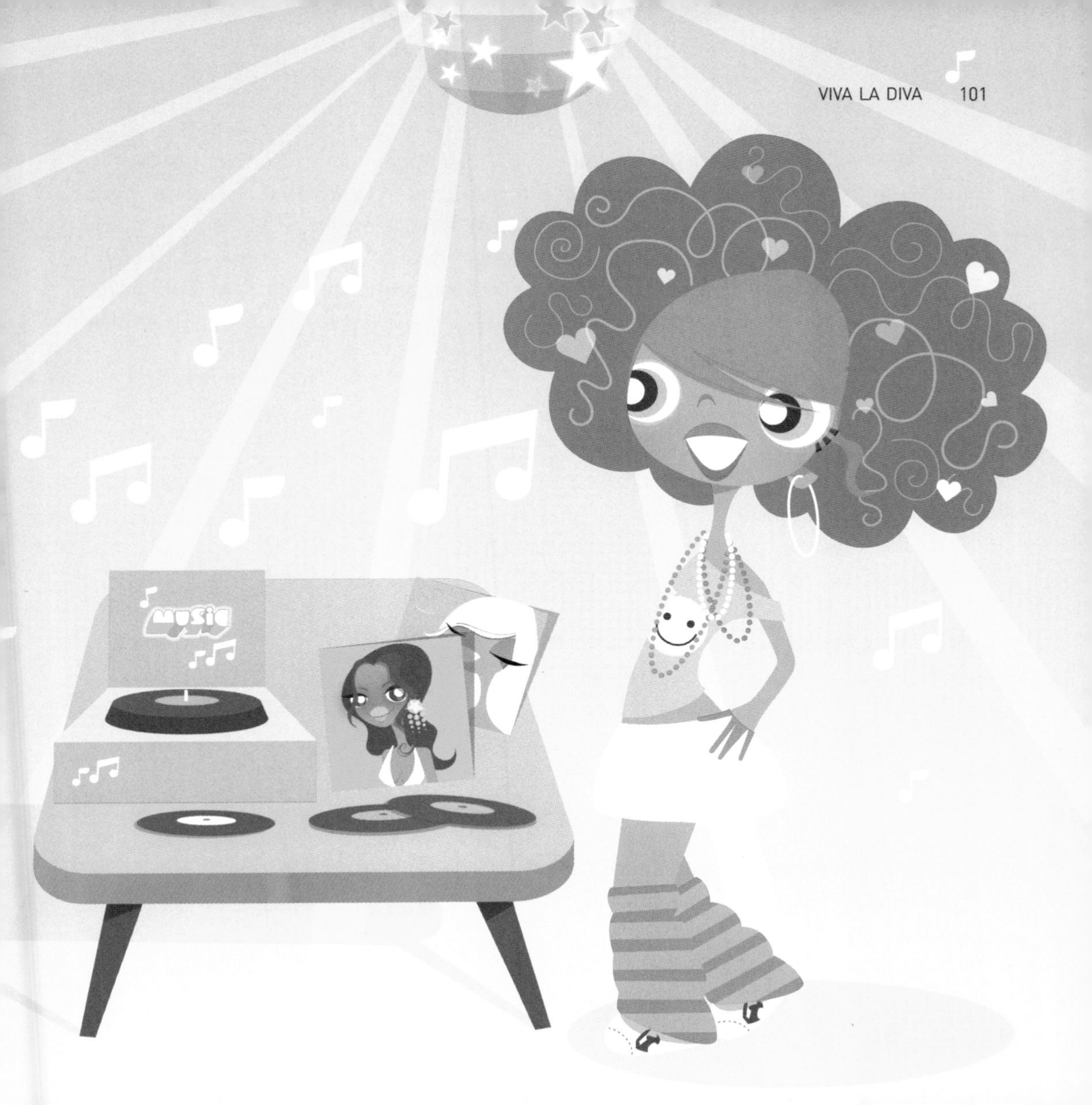
Music

Throwing back your duvet each morning cues your opening credits... What better way to start them rolling than with a press of the 'play' button to start your personal Viva la Diva play list? And even if you don't have access to your own mp3 player, you always have access to the sparkly pink ghetto blaster in your mind... (mine is constantly playing different girly themed songs as I strut my stuff through town. It's always fabulous to know that the power of Gwen Stefani is always with me... mp3 player or not.)

What is your theme song?

....
....
....
....
....

Which song makes you jump-in-the-air happy?

....
....
....
....
....

Which song makes you cry an entire river?

....
....
....

What was the first cd you ever bought?

....

....

....

....

....

"...DON'T STAND IN THE CORNER, WAITING FOR A CHANCE... MAKE YOUR OWN MUSIC, START YOUR OWN DANCE..." **Madonna from Spotlight**

Hearing a tune we love can make us feel happy, make us weepy, trigger fabulous-o memories, make us throw shapes, and turn an otherwise borin', snorin' day into one filled with neon disco-glitter rainbows.

Your very own Viva la Diva soundtrack should be filled with anything that inspires you to create, throw shapes on the dance-floor and do lip-synch routines whilst jumping on your bed!

List your Viva La Diva soundtrack picks

....

....

....

....

....

....

....

....

....

....

If you had a band, what would you name it?

....

....

....

....

....

....

....

....

....

....

Showtime!

Li'l miss Fabulous, it's your time to shine and to prepare you for super-sparkly life in the pink-tinted spotlight.

Any Pink Thinkin' Diva will tell you that you need to carefully plan and think about the PERFECT message you're going to send out to the world about you and your ah-mazing potential.

Model-girls have portfolios, and actress-types have showreels - basically, these are the key ways to showcase their talent and to prove to their potential bosses how great they are. Cool, huh?

Why don't you create your very own Viva La Diva Scrapbook of Fabness? Fill it up with all the the things that make you YOU-nique, pop in pictures of yourself working your best outfit, create a tagline for yourself, stick in pictures of people you love who inspire you, pictures of things you'd like in your life, make a list of all the things that make you stand out from the crowd - your Viva La Diva scrapbook of Fabness will be a constant visual reminder of your very own Viva La Diva message!

The Pink Ladies and I have put together our must-have, Viva la Diva goody bag to ensure total star-shaped diva status, pronto!

Picture perfect

Angel's Viva La Diva snapshot tips to perfect pics – every time!

* Practise your smile – rehearse in front of a mirror, or do a test run (think Alicia Silverstone in Clueless) with a digi camera for instant results.
* Don't go in front of the camera without a beauty check. Wayward curls, smudged lips and food in your teeth are a guaranteed photo disaster.
* Don't pose. If you concentrate on something other than the lens – the cutie in your class perhaps – you'll look more relaxed.
* Turn sideways. Facing the camera head-on makes you appear broader than you really are.
* If you tend to close your eyes in every pic, try this blink-free strategy: shut your eyes and ask the photographer to count down from three before clicking the shutter. On three, open up and smile.
* To avoid looking scared or surprised, don't stare directly into the camera. Instead, focus your eyes just above it or over the photographer's shoulder.

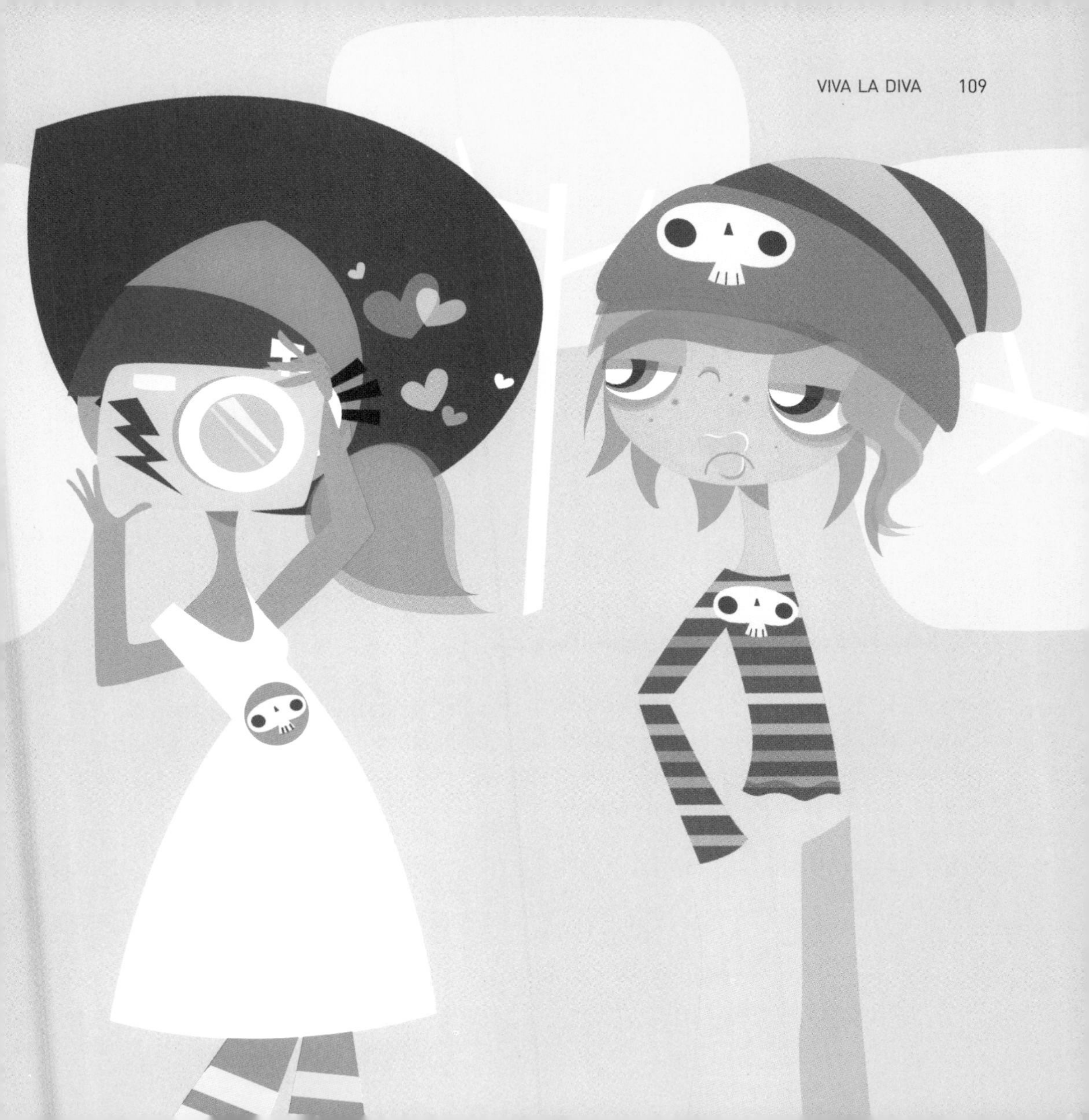

Get the edge

Pink thinkin' divas are cool. Fact.

And the best bit is, they don't need the whole world to confirm it, because genuine coolness comes from within, chica. If you can look in the mirror and tell yourself 'I'm fabulous', it really doesn't matter what anyone else thinks.

What do you tell yourself when you look in the mirror? Make it sweet, make it positive and repeat it to yourself everyday!

....

....

....

....

They have belly-fire passion...

There's nothing cooler than a girl who isn't afraid to go after what she wants in life. For belly-fire passion props, check out Oscar-winningdirector girl Sophia Coppola. Sophia is fabulous-o at what she does and is passionate about it too - how else do you explain the masterpiece that is Marie Antoinette?

What's your belly-fire passion?

....

....

....

....

They're willing to take a risk...

Taking risks is all part of being a pink thinkin' diva.

The familiar, the ordinary and everything that's been done before is just... well, boring.

Innovation = diva-like coolness.

What risk could you take today to make your life sweeter?

....
....
....
....
....

They're one-of-a-kind...

Pink thinkin' divas don't follow, they lead, because being an individual is so much cooler than being a carbon copy version of your best gal pal.

What trend are you going to set?

....
....
....
....
....
....

They've got their own sense of style...

I heart 1950s glamour, Angel works bright red lipstick, Bella wears heels on a daily basis and Sadie works quirky-cute beautifully. We each have a signature look that we love and know works for us. The key to looking feisty, fun, fearless and fabulous is dressing yourself in what makes you feel chic and comfy at the same time. And once you find it, don't be afraid to go with it.

What's your signature look?

....
....
....
....
....
....
....

They don't actually care if they're cool...

Being cool doesn't really rate on a pink thinkin' diva's radar. As weird as it sounds, the moment you stop caring if you're cool or not, is the moment you actually become it. **If you didn't care about how cool you looked, what one thing would you do?**

....
....
....
....
....

Being a Diva is Sweet

Being a feisty fun, fearless and fabulous pink thinkin' diva = a recipe for a sweet, sweet life!

Now, I dig a make-up bag full of fabulous products and a wardrobe full of I-totally-needed-them-at-the-time purchases as much as the next chica, but these things do not make me jump-in-the-air-happy.

Nah–uh.

Why?

Because when you're a pink thinkin' diva, as fun as it is to work the outside fabulousity, it's about working the WHOLE package – inside and out!

Take Eva Satine for example. This Negative Nina is as pretty-as-a-picture but she's got the most twisted and ugly insides with the most vicious, poison-spitting tongue.

Who would want to live their life like that?

While Eva may get her kicks giving the cast of Mean Girls a run for their money, she has zilcho respect for herself and others: she smokes – ick and she trash-talks anyone that isn't in her clique.

These are NOT the ingredients for a sweet pink thinkin' diva life.

These however, are:

Be true to yourself – living by your own set of pink thinkin' values and tuning in to your inner 'li'l miss fabulous' voice (the one that tells you how great you are and knows right from wrong instinctively) is a one-way ticket to sweetsville.
If you live life according to your own pink thinkin' rulebook every day, and don't try to live by someone else's, you will be happier x 100.

Fact.

My top three life values are – kindness, honesty and compassion, what are yours?

....

....

....

....

....

Take care of yourself – Have you ever been in a foot-stompin' mad mood because you've spent the entire weekend studying with only a family sized packet of jaffa cakes and a bar of chocolate to keep you company?

Er...Me too.

There is a pink thinkin' diva cure, it involves movin, snoozin' and eating nutritious food. Start with exercise - it doesn't have to be boring y'know, not if you exercise like a kid! Two easy-peasy, inexpensive ways to exercise are hula hoping and skipping. I don't love the exercising but I love child's play – you can hula-hoop your way through an episode of your favourite soap or skip in your backgarden – happy days!

Snoozin' is mucho important, so make sure you get an eight-hour fix. It will give your bod time to rest and repair, and is by far the best beauty tip you'll ever get.

Finally, while chocolate is yumsum x 100 in moderation, you'll have muchos more energy if you swap the calorie-laden biscuits and choc and snack on fruit, veggies, yoghurt and dee-lish nuts instead.

How do you keep your sweet self is in tip-top, tutti-frutti condition?

....
....
....
....
....
....
....

Show your love – Remind yourself of ALL the good and ah-mazing things in your life every day. In fact, why not kick-start each day with your very own sweet pink thinkin' diva life list?

Take note of the things you love that make your life great – your mum's cupcakes, the smell of rain, your best bud... because showing kindness is showing you want others to be happy, too.

Sweet.

Lola's sweet pink thinkin' diva life list

- ☆ **The Pink Ladies** – because they let me know I'm loved and cared for EVERY day
- ☆ **The rainbow after a downpour** – I heart rainbows
- ☆ **The lollipop lady** - she throws me a smile every day, whatever the weather
- ☆ **Fresh laundry** – I love the smell of new sheets on my bed – ahhhhhh!
- ☆ **My ability to accessorise** – because no matter how bad the outfit, I know I can work it with a string of pink plastic beads!

What's on your sweet pink thinkin' diva life list?

....

....

....

....

....

....

....

....

....

....

....

....

....

....

....

See it to believe it

There really is no better time than NOW to bust out the kick-ass, too-cool-for-school version of your sweet self.

Well, that is, if you had the guts to go through with it, right?

Being a pink thinkin' diva is all about being confident – if you don't believe that you've got it going on, (pssst – chica, you totally have, y'know) it's time to revamp your 'tude to a pink thinkin' diva 'tude, sweet thing!

Have you ever heard that saying 'I'll believe it when I see it'?

Well, pink thinkin' divas flick the switch to 'reverse' and see it to believe it!

It goes a li'l something like this – if a pink thinkin' diva wants something – like, to do well in an exam or to walk into a party on her own with kick-ass confidence – she'll imagine herself doing well at it, she'll see images in her mind and then she'll make them come true. If you add a touch of concentration, and a lot of feelings, it becomes a super-huge pink thinkin' collaboration of fabulousness that actually makes things happen.

It's like daydreaming, sprinkled with magic, pink glitter sparkles – tell me, what's not to love about that?

So, how does it work?

The 'see it to believe it' technique can be used whatever your scenario, it's good like that, but for now, imagine that you want to be a muchos confident girl on your first day back at school after the summer hols...

⭐ Find yourself somewhere comfy where you won't be disturbed, then lay back, close your eyes and start to picture your first day back at school like a super cool teen movie starring you.

⭐ Choose a killah feel-good theme tune - mine is peroxide blonde, girl duo Shampoo's power anthem: Girl Power. Then imagine you're walking tall in the playground, people are smiling and talking to you, you're smiling and talking back – you're looking fab, you're feeling fab – it's the perfect opening scene.

☆ Add lots of colour, make it as vibrant and as real as you possibly can, listen to what people are saying – if they're paying you compliments what are they saying?

☆ Now replay it. The more you replay the opening scene in your mind, the more natural it will feel when you put it into action later.

By mentally rehearsing an event or seeing yourself as a super confident version of your sweet self, you create a permanent hard copy of success that is uploaded to your brain's computer.

So, when it comes to putting the action into practise, you'll be 100% sure in your mind that you can do it and that you're confident.

Cool eh?

The next step is to do it.

My secret?

Faking celeb-style confidence.

Those celeb-types totally know how to work it – and this is your movie remember, and you're the star, so walk with your head up and your shoulders back, and look people in the eye when you're talking to them.

Once you've learned how to fake a-list cool, you'll look and feel it in no time!

Ah-mazing affirmations

Positive self-talk, or affirmations, are one of the most powerful tools in any pink thinkin' diva's vanity case! When your head is messy and stressy, they can boost and protect your self-esteem mucho much!

Affirmations don't have to be anything fancy schmancy, a simple one to five word affirmation works the best. "Yes, I can do this." Works wonders when you are faced with a brand spankin' new challenge.

As tempting as it might be to use affirmations to deal with all your hassles at once, if you do a million trillion each morning, guaranteed they'll lose their kick.

So, write a list of all the things that are making your head stressy and put the nastiest, most stressy at the top...

....

....

....

....

....

....

....

....

....

....

Now, create an affirmation that will flip the way you normally think about your number one head stresser.

If you're not sure where to start, ask yourself 'If I could change just one thing about my life, what would it be?'

Creating affirmations

Here's what you're going to do. There are an infinite number of affirmations – the only limit is your imagination! The most important thing is they must always be phrased in the most pink-thinkin' positive way possible. If the message of an affirmation doesn't seem right to you, it won't work for you.

If you say: 'OH I HAVEN'T GOT ENOUGH TIME TO DO MY HOMEWORK;' 'THERE'S NOT ENOUGH TIME IN THE DAY'

Say this instead: We all have the same amount of time, it's just that some people seem to manage it better than others. So instead of saying 'I HAVEN'T GOT THE TIME' say, 'I CAN FIND THE TIME FOR EVERYTHING THAT'S IMPORTANT FOR ME RIGHT NOW.' You'll start to see how the choice of words you use is muchos important.

If you say this: 'I'M NOT A CONFIDENT PERSON.'

Say this instead: When people say 'I'M NOT VERY CONFIDENT; I'M SHY', they then automatically feel shy and lack confidence. If you say 'NOT CONFIDENT', if you say 'SHY', if you act shy and retiring, what types of results are you going to get? Not the ones you want, that's for sure, gorgeous girl.

What if, instead, you created a new affirmation, one that is empowering and makes you feel feisty and fabulous? Something like. 'I HAVE ALL THE CONFIDENCE THAT I NEED RIGHT NOW'.

Whatever your head stresser, create an affirmation that will inspire and motivate you. Become your own motivational speaker. Write it on a post-it note and pin it somewhere you look everyday, write it in your diary, say it to yourself first thing in the morning, on the bus, in the bath anywhere and everywhere and as often as possible.

Keep affirmations short, simple and in the present tense.

Here's some you might like to use:

If you're a creative girl in need of a boost, say: "…I AM TALENTED AND CREATIVE…"

If you're working at learning a new skill or language, say: "…I AM IMPROVING EVERY DAY IN EVERY WAY…"

If you find it difficult to make tough decisions, say: "…I AM A CONFIDENT AND GREAT DECISION MAKER…"

What are your ah-mazing affirmations?

....

....

....

....

....

....

....

....

....

....

....

....

....

YOUR DIVA CONTRACT

I, ...am officially a pink-thinkin' Diva!

I never, evah want to be a blend-in girl so I celebrate being YOU-nique on a daily basis!

I'm the star of my movie - lights, camera...ACTION!

I know my own mind and set my standards high. Why? Because I'm worth it!

I give and receive compliments as if they're sugar-coated candy goodness!

I punch the air and scream 'Viva La Diva' because I'm me, and I rock and rule!

SIGNED BY ••••••••••••••••••••••••••••

angel

bella